New Canaan Library

151 Main Street
New Canaan, CT 06840

(203)801-BOOK
www.newcanaanlibrary.org

The Countries

Brazil

Kate A. Furlong
ABDO Publishing Company

visit us at
www.abdopub.com

Published by ABDO Publishing Company, 4940 Viking Drive, Edina, Minnesota 55435. Copyright © 2001 by Abdo Consulting Group, Inc. International copyrights reserved in all countries. No part of this book may be reproduced in any form without written permission from the publisher.

Printed in the United States.

Photo Credits: Corbis

Contributing Editors: Bob Italia, Tamara L. Britton, and Christine Fournier
Art Direction & Maps: Neil Klinepier

Library of Congress Cataloging-in-Publication Data

Furlong, Kate A., 1977-
   Brazil / Kate A. Furlong.
      p. cm. -- (The countries)
   ISBN 1-57765-491-9
   1. Brazil--Juvenile literature. [1.Brazil.] I. Title. II. Series.

F2508.5 .F87 2001
981--dc21

00-050264

Contents

Oi! 4
Fast Facts 6
Timeline 7
Brazil's Past 8
A Land of Plenty 12
Wild Things 18
Brazilians 20
Earning a Living 26
Colorful Cities 28
From Here to There 30
Brazil's Government 32
Brazilian Celebrations 34
Fun in Brazil 36
Glossary 38
Web Sites 39
Index 40

Oi!

Hello from Brazil! Brazil is a large country in South America. It has vast, undeveloped rain forests. The rain forests are home to thousands of plants and animals.

Most Brazilians live in large cities. They make goods to export to other countries. They also work in service jobs. Brazilians who live in the country may work as farmers or miners.

Brazilians are a mix of Europeans, Africans, and Indians. Over time, they have joined together to form a Brazilian **culture**. Its music is world famous. Its artists are honored. And its food is delicious.

For years, Portugal ruled Brazil. After Brazil gained independence, **dictators** ruled the country. Then the military took control. Today, Brazilians elect their leaders. These leaders are working to make Brazil a great place to work and live.

Oi *from Brazil!*

Fast Facts

OFFICIAL NAME: Federal Republic of Brazil (República Federativa do Brasil)
CAPITAL: Brasília

LAND
- Highest Peak: Pico da Neblina 1,000 feet (3,014m)
- Major River: Amazon River

PEOPLE
- Population: 172,860,370 (2000 est.)
- Major Cities: São Paulo, Rio de Janeiro
- Official Language: Portuguese
- Religion: Catholicism, African-based religions

GOVERNMENT
- Form: Federal Republic
- Head of Government: President
- Legislature: National Congress (made up of the Federal Senate and the Chamber of Deputies)
- Flag: Green with a large yellow diamond in the center; the diamond bears a globe with a banner and stars; the banner has the national motto (Order and Progress); the stars represent Brazil's states and provinces.
- Nationhood: September 7, 1822

ECONOMY
- Agricultural Products: Coffee, soybeans, wheat, rice, corn, sugarcane, cocoa, citrus fruit, and bananas
- Mining Products: Bauxite, gold, iron ore, manganese, nickel, phosphates, platinum, tin, and uranium
- Manufactured Products: Textiles, shoes, chemicals, cement, lumber, iron ore, tin, steel, aircraft, and motor vehicles
- Money: Real (one real equals 100 centavos)

Brazil's Flag

Brazil's money is called the Real (HAY-ow). Many bills are called Reais (HAY-ice).

Timeline

1500	Portuguese arrive in Brazil
1821	Dom Pedro rules Brazil
1822	Dom Pedro declares independence for Brazil
1841	Dom Pedro II rules Brazil
1888	Slavery ends
1889	Military overtakes government; Brazil becomes a republic
1930	Getúlio Vargas takes control of government
1951	Getúlio Vargas elected president
1960	Brasília is completed and becomes Brazil's new capital
1964	Military overtakes government
1973	Yanomami first meet Brazilians
1989	Brazil holds its first democratic elections since 1964

Red-eyed tree frogs live in the rain forest.

Brazil's Past

People first **migrated** to North America about 15,000 years ago. Many of them moved south to present-day Brazil. The Tupí (too-PEE) are Brazil's most famous native tribe.

In 1500, the Tupí greeted a large ship off the coast. It had Portuguese sailors on it. They were led by Pedro Álvares Cabral (PAY-droh AL-var-ess ca-BRAHL). Cabral claimed the Tupí's land for Portugal. Portugal called its new land Terra de Vera Cruz (TEHR-ah day VEHR-ah KHROOZ). Its name soon changed to Brazil.

Many Portuguese moved to Brazil. They found that the soil was good for growing **sugarcane**. Settlers built sugarcane plantations. They used Brazil's natives as slaves on the plantations. But many of the native slaves died. So the Portuguese began to use Africans as slaves.

Brazil's plantations quickly became successful. So other countries wanted to add Brazil to their empires. French and Dutch soldiers attacked Brazil in the hope of overtaking it.

Despite the attacks, Portugal remained in control of Brazil. In 1821, Portugal's king put his son Dom Pedro (dohm PAY-droh) in charge of Brazil. On September 7, 1822, Dom Pedro declared Brazil's independence. Portugal agreed to make Brazil an independent country. Dom Pedro became Brazil's first emperor.

Dom Pedro was a poor leader. So his son, Dom Pedro II, became emperor in 1841. Dom Pedro II ruled for nearly 50 years. He strengthened the **parliament** and encouraged people to move to Brazil. And in 1888, he ended slavery.

Pedro Álvares Cabral

Dom Pedro II

In 1889, the military overthrew Dom Pedro II. They made Brazil a **republic**. The military ruled Brazil for four years. Then it turned the government over to the people.

In 1930, Getúlio Vargas (szuh-TOO-lee-oh VAHR-ghus) overtook the government. He ruled as a **dictator** for the next 20 years. Vargas tried to build Brazil's industry. He tried to improve the cities, too. In 1951, he was officially elected president.

In 1964, the military overtook Brazil's government once again. This is called the Revolution of 1964. Many Brazilians disliked the new government. It killed and tortured people who spoke out against it. And it forbade political parties.

Brazilians started protesting. The military returned the government to the citizens. In 1989, Brazil held

democratic elections. These were the first such elections since the military took control in 1964.

Today, Brazil faces many challenges. It owes other countries much money. Some of its important leaders are **corrupt**. And some people don't have good food, water, or homes. But the people are pulling together. They want to fix Brazil's problems and make it an even stronger nation.

Getúlio Vargas

A Land of Plenty

Brazil is a large country. It covers about half of South America. Brazil borders every South American country except Ecuador and Chile. Eastern Brazil borders the Atlantic Ocean.

Brazil's Atlantic coast is home to the country's major cities, such as Rio de Janeiro.

North America
Europe
Asia
Africa
South America
DETAIL AREA
Australia
Antarctica

Columbia
Venezuela
French Guiana
Guyana
Suriname
Peru
BRAZIL
Bolivia
Chile
Paraguay
ATLANTIC OCEAN
Argentina
Uruguay

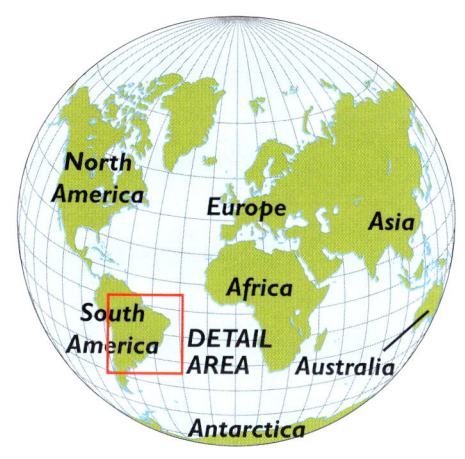

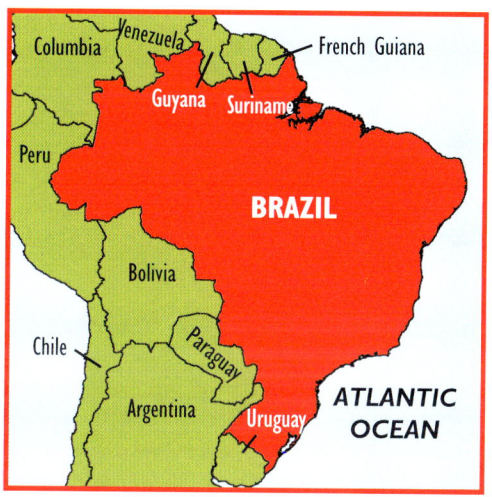

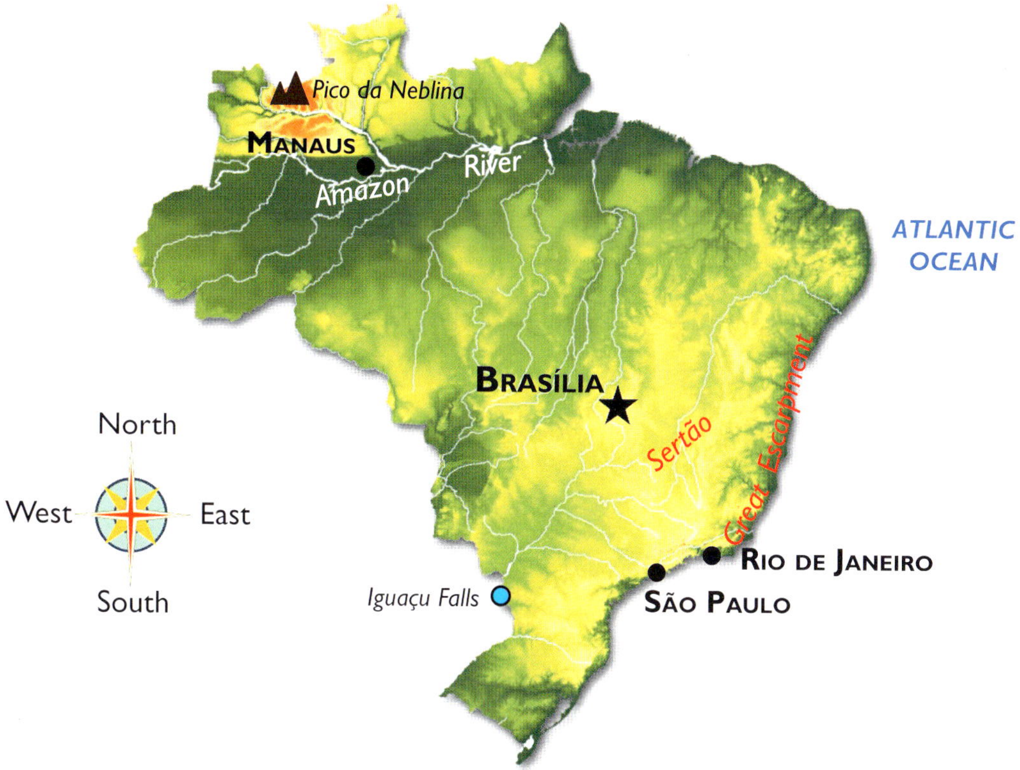
Pico da Neblina
MANAUS
River
Amazon
ATLANTIC OCEAN
BRASÍLIA
North
West
East
South
Sertão
Great Escarpment
RIO DE JANEIRO
SÃO PAULO
Iguaçu Falls

Northwestern Brazil is called the Amazon Region. It is hot, humid, and rainy. Many rivers flow through the Amazon Region. The largest one is called the Amazon River. In the far north, there are mountains. One is called Pico da Neblina (PEE-coh dah nehb-LEE-nah). It is Brazil's highest peak.

Recently, Brazilians have been clearing the Amazon rain forest. But this hurts the environment. People around the world are working to save the rain forest.

The Amazon River

A Land of Plenty **15**

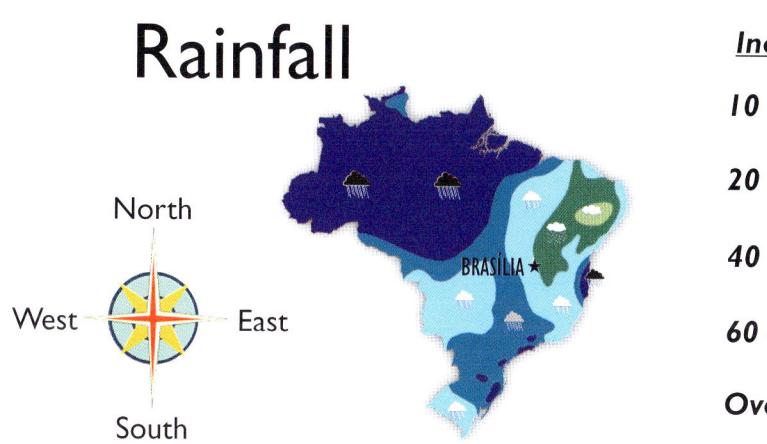

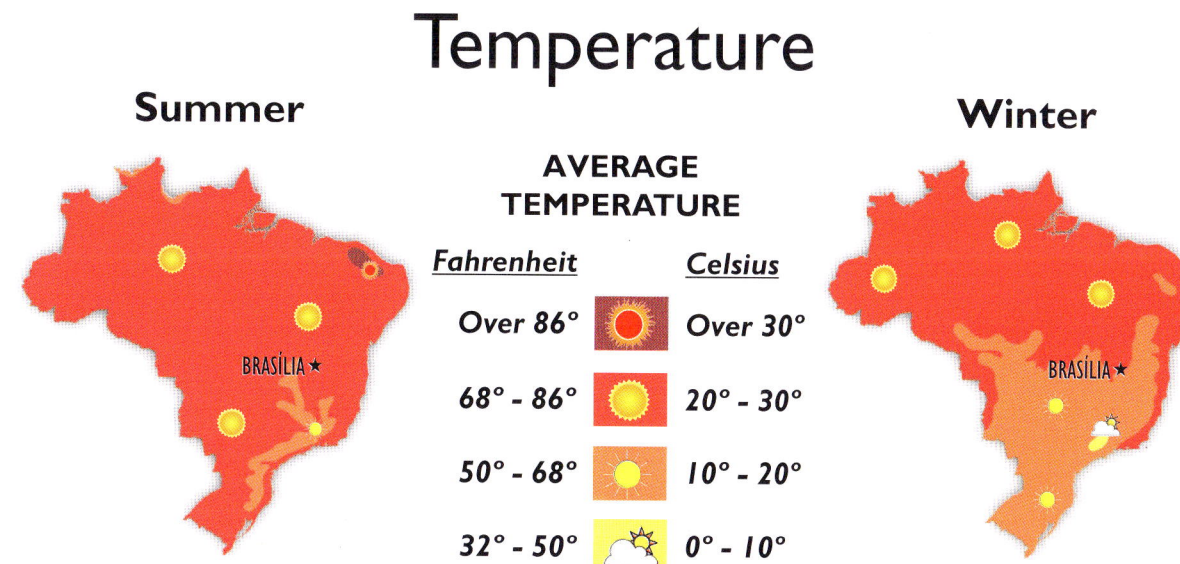

The Atlantic Ocean borders eastern Brazil. The land near the coast has rich soil. It is hot and gets plenty of rain. The land away from the coast is called the *sertão* (SEHR-tow). It is flat and has poor soil. The *sertão* is hot and gets very little rain.

Central and southern Brazil have flat, grassy plains. This area has Brazil's best farmland. Along the coast, there is a steep cliff called the Great Escarpment (es-KAHRP-muhnt). The weather is warm and there is plenty of rain.

Brazil's land is known for its beauty. One of its most famous sites is Iguaçu (e-gwah-SOO) Falls. It is a series of waterfalls in southern Brazil. The falls drop 262 feet (80 m) and are more than 2 miles (3 km) wide.

Opposite page: Iguaçu Falls

Wild Things

Brazil's Amazon rain forest has more kinds of plants than anywhere else on Earth. One acre in the Amazon rain forest may have more than 250 kinds of trees. There are also mosses, orchids, and other kinds of plants.

Brazil's land is home to numerous animals. Many kinds of monkeys live in the treetops. Sloths live in the trees, too. They are mammals with round faces, long tails, and sharp claws. Brazil is also home to the capybara. It is the world's largest **rodent**. It can weigh up to 110 pounds (27 kg).

Brazil's waters also have many animals. Anaconda snakes live in the water. They can grow to 16 feet (5 m) long. Jacaré (szuh-carh-EH) also live in Brazil's waters. They look like alligators.

Wild Things 19

Brazil is home to hundreds of kinds of birds. They live all over the country. In the rain forest, there are parrots, toucans, and hawks. Storks, parakeets, cardinals, finches, ibises, and cuckoos live near the swamps.

Brazil's waters are full of fish. Piranhas have strong jaws and large, sharp teeth.

Brazilians

Brazil has been home to many kinds of people. Indians, Portuguese, Africans, and **immigrants** from Europe and Asia have called Brazil home. Today, most Brazilians are a mix of all these groups.

The Amazon Region is home to a native people called the Yanomami (YAHN-oh-MAHM-ee). They lived all by themselves deep in the rain forest. In 1973, the Yanomami first met Brazilians. The Brazilians were using Yanomami land for a new highway. Today, the Yanomami live on **reservations**. They continue to follow their traditional ways.

Nearly all Brazilians speak Portuguese. It is Brazil's official language. Some native peoples still speak their traditional languages. The most commonly spoken native language is Tupí-Guaraní (too-PEE gwah-rah-NEE).

Brazilians 21

A group of Yanomami gathers food in the rain forest.

Many Brazilians are Catholic. But Brazil has many other religions, too. These religions combine African and Brazilian folk beliefs with Christianity. One such religion is called Candomblé. It mixes African gods and Catholic saints.

Most Brazilian families live in tall apartment buildings. Poor families live in areas called *favelas* (fah-VELL-ahs). They have shacks made out of tin and cardboard. They have no electricity or running water. Rich families live in large homes. They have tall fences and guards for protection.

Families in the Amazon live in traditional houses. They are built of saplings or **sugarcane** stalks. Some homes are round with thatched roofs. Some round homes are large. They can hold up to 100 people.

A favela in Rio de Janeiro

Biscoitos de Maizena

Biscoitos de Maizena are delicious Brazilian cookies. The main ingredient is cornstarch. The brand name for cornstarch in Brazil is Maizena. That is how the cookies got their name.

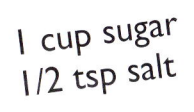

2 cups cornstarch
1 egg
1 1/2 stick butter
1 cup sugar
1/2 tsp salt

Preheat oven to 375° F. Mix the dry ingredients. Add the egg and butter. Knead well. Let the dough stand for fifteen minutes. Form the dough into small balls. Put the balls on a cookie sheet. Flatten them with a fork. Bake for seven minutes.

AN IMPORTANT NOTE TO THE CHEF: Always have an adult help with the preparation and cooking of food. Never use kitchen utensils or appliances without adult permission and supervision.

English	Portuguese
Yes	Sim
No	Não
Thank You	Obrigado/a
Please	Por favor
Hello	Oi
Goodbye	Tchau

Fresh fruit, beef, and seafood are popular foods in Brazil. Most people eat fruit, coffee, and rolls for breakfast. Lunch is the largest meal of the day. People often eat meat, black beans, and rice. Dinner is similar to lunch, except it is not so large. Dinner is usually eaten late at night.

Brazil's government provides free public schools. And the Catholic Church offers many private schools. But two out of ten Brazilians do not finish elementary school. Instead, they must work to help their families. Some cities have night schools for children who must work during the day.

Students who finish elementary school can attend a *colégio* (cohl-EH-szee-oh). It is like high school in the U.S. or Canada. After finishing *colégio*, some students attend a university.

Opposite page: Children working in a small group with their teacher

Earning a Living

Many Brazilians work as farmers. They supply the world with several kinds of foods. Brazil is the world's leading producer of coffee, **sugarcane**, soybeans, papayas, oranges, and cassavas. Brazil exports many of these products to other countries.

Brazilians have been mining their land for many years. The land is rich in minerals. Brazil is a leading producer of iron. It also has important sources of coal, salt, copper, gold, and diamonds.

Manufacturing goods has created jobs for many Brazilians. They make cars, trucks, and airplanes. They also make clothing, **textiles**, and leather goods. Most manufacturing is done in Brazil's largest cities.

Tourism has become a growing part of Brazil's **economy**. So companies are building new hotels, restaurants, and resorts for visitors. This has created new jobs for Brazilians.

Many Brazilian farmers sell their crops at open-air markets.

Colorful Cities

São Paulo (SAHO PAW-loh) is located on Brazil's southeast coast. It is Brazil's largest city. About 20 million people live there. It has skyscrapers and large freeways. It also has many museums, libraries, theaters, and beaches.

Rio de Janeiro (REE-oh day jehn-EHR-oh) is Brazil's second-largest city. It is often just called Rio. About 7 million people live there. For many years, Rio served as Brazil's capital.

Rio also has two of the world's most beautiful beaches, Copacabana and Ipanema. And a famous statue called Christ the Redeemer sits atop the Corcovado mountain and watches over the city.

The capital of Brazil is called Brasília (brah-SEEL-ee-ah). About 2 million Brazilians live there. It is located

Colorful Cities **29**

in Brazil's interior. Builders started constructing Brasília in 1957. It took only three years to finish. In 1960, Brazil's capital moved from Rio de Janeiro to Brasília.

Copacabana Beach

From Here to There

Brazil has a large system of roads. They connect local towns and large cities. The roads are full of cars, trucks, taxis, motorcycles, and buses. Most Brazilians take a bus to work or school.

São Paulo and Rio de Janeiro have subway systems called metrôs (MEHT-rohs). Brazil's metrôs are fast, clean, and safe. They are an easy way for Brazilians to get around the biggest cities.

All of Brazil's large cities have airports. There are flights to cities within Brazil. Brazil also has flights to other countries. And visitors can even take a small plane to the Amazon rain forest.

The Amazon's thick jungle makes traveling difficult. Most people travel by boat on the Amazon River. Its main port is Manaus (mahn-AWSE). The Amazon also

From Here to There 31

has a major highway running through it. It is called Transamazônica (trans-ahma-ZOHN-ee-ka) Highway.

Many cars, trucks, and buses crowd the streets of São Paulo.

Brazil's Government

Brazil is a federal **republic**. It has 26 states plus a federal district in Brasília. Brazil's government follows the **constitution** of 1988. It divides Brazil's power between the president, the lawmakers, and the courts.

Brazilians elect a president every five years. He or she is the head of state. The president works with other countries, helps pass laws, and makes sure the nation is protected.

Brazilians elect lawmakers to serve in the National Congress. The Congress rules on treaties with other countries. They allow the president to declare war. And they make sure Brazil's states are doing well.

Brazil's highest court is called the Federal Superior Court. It is made up of 33 judges. Brazil's president names the judges to the court. The judges rule on issues related to the whole nation. Other courts rule on local matters.

Brazil's Government 33

The National Congress building in Brasília

Brazilian Celebrations

Brazil's biggest festival is called Carnival. It is a four-day celebration before **Lent**. Brazilians dress in flashy costumes, watch parades, and dance in the street. Brazil's largest and most famous Carnival celebration is in Rio de Janeiro.

At Christmas, Brazilian families set up **Nativity scenes** called *presepios* (press-EHP-ee-ohs). They also decorate a Christmas tree. On Christmas Eve, many Brazilians go to a midnight **mass**. Then Papai Noel (pahp-EYE nohel) brings gifts to the children.

Some people celebrate Iemanjá (ehm-ahn-YAH). Iemanjá is an African goddess of the oceans. People begin their celebrations at night on December 31. They throw flowers and perfume into the sea. They sing and dance on the beach until dawn.

A Carnival parade in Rio de Janeiro

Fun in Brazil

Brazil's warm, sunny weather allows people to spend much time outside. The country's many beaches are often full of young people. They like to relax, sunbathe, and play sports on the beach.

Soccer is Brazil's national sport. Brazilians of all ages enjoy playing and watching soccer. Brazil's most famous soccer player is Pelé (PAY-LAY). Many people say he is the world's best player. In 22 years of playing soccer, he won 53 titles.

Music is also important in Brazilian life. The samba is a kind of Brazilian music with African roots. Bossa nova is a type of Brazilian music that began in the 1950s. It mixes jazz with other Brazilian rhythms. Bossa nova and samba music have become world famous.

Brazil has a long history of art. Its most famous painter is Cândido Portinari (cahn-DEE-doh pohr-tehn-AHR-ee). He only painted Brazil and its people. His best-known painting is called *Coffee*. It shows workers on a Brazilian coffee plantation.

Brazil's artists, musicians, and soccer players have brought Brazil into the spotlight. Their country is rich in people and natural resources. Brazilians are working hard to make sure they carry Brazil's wonderful **culture** into the future.

Pelé juggles a soccer ball

Glossary

constitution - a paper that describes a country's laws and government.
corrupt - someone who is influenced by other people to be dishonest.
culture - the customs, arts, and tools of a nation or people at a certain time.
democracy - a form of government where the people hold the power. They elect officials to represent them.
dictator - a ruler who has complete control and usually governs in a cruel or unfair way.
economy - the way a state or nation uses its money, goods, and natural resources.
immigrant - a person who comes into a foreign country to live.
Lent - the 40 weekdays before Easter.
mass - a worship celebration in the Catholic Church.
migrate - to move from one country or region to settle in another.
Nativity scene - a scene from the birth of Jesus.
parliament - the highest lawmaking body in a country.
republic - a type of government in which the power rests with voting citizens and is carried out by elected officials.
reservation - land set apart by the government for a certain purpose.
rodent - any of several related animals that have large front teeth for gnawing.
sugarcane - a tall grass with thick, juicy stems from which sugar is made.
textile - of or having to do with the designing, manufacturing, or producing of woven fabric.

Web Sites

Rainforest Alliance
http://www.rainforest-alliance.org/kids&teachers/index.html
This fun, colorful site is sponsored by the Rainforest Alliance. Click on the frog pictures for great information on frogs of the rainforest. Download photos of rainforest animals to color, play games, and more!

Brazil Soccer
http://www.brazilfutbol.com
Learn about Brazil, read the history of the World Cup, and catch up on soccer news at this site from the Brazil Football Federation.

These sites are subject to change. Go to your favorite search engine and type in "Brazil" for more sites.

Index

A
Amazon Region 14, 18, 20, 22, 30, 31
Amazon River 14, 30
animals 4, 18, 19
art 4, 37

B
Brasília 28, 29, 32

C
Cabral, Pedro Álvares 8
children 24
climate 14, 16, 36

E
economy 4, 8, 9, 10, 26
education 24

F
festivals 34
food 4, 11, 24, 26

G
geography 4, 12, 14, 16
government 4, 9, 10, 11, 24, 32
Great Escarpment 16

H
holidays 34
homes 11, 22

I
Iguaçu Falls 16
industry 26

L
language 20

M
manufacturing 26
mining 26
music 4, 36

P
Pedro, Dom 9
Pedro II, Dom 9, 10
Pelé 36

Pico da Neblina 14
plants 4, 18
Portinari, Cândido 37

R
rain forest 4, 14, 18, 19, 20, 30
religion 21, 24, 34
Rio de Janeiro 28, 29, 30, 34

S
São Paulo 28, 30
sertão 16
slavery 8, 9
sports 36

T
tourism 26
transportation 20, 30, 31
Tupí 8

V
Vargas, Getúlio 10

Y
Yanomami 20